MOODS

MOODS

PROSE POEMS

BY

Mercedes de Acosta

QUALE PRESS

Afterword copyright © 2025 by Kathryn Good-Schiff

ISBN: 978-1-935835-38-7 trade paperback edition

First edition (introduction and prose poems)
published in 1919 by Moffat, Yard & Co.

LCCN: 2025949211

Cover: *Le bal élégant, la danse à la campagne,*
painting by Marie Laurencin, 1913

Author photo from 1919/20 by Arthur Genthe

A ClearSound book from
Quale Press

www.quale.com

CONTENTS

INTRODUCTION

There is a happy gift revealed in these little pastels, vignettes, or whatever one wishes to name such fragments that Miss de Acosta has written and which refuse to be catalogued and classified. They stand out in one's reading in refreshing contrast to many opaque books of verse. They are not poetry; but they are the most singable prose, and they have a haunting quality, a breath of mystery, as though a ghost walked in a garden. They are strange, but they are human too; for if Miss de Acosta has anything it is a belief in, and an understanding of, her fellow human beings. In the little picture of the tired woman in the subway she shows with what feeling her heart is charged; and in the fragment of the studio, the climax is deftly approached. Brief as these glimpses of human experience are, they leave one with a sense of finality. It is as though a door were suddenly opened, or a window quickly raised — and then as suddenly closed again. But one has seen the room in its entirety, and the interior has been photographed on the brain.

Miss de Acosta, who comes forward here with her first volume, bears promise of even finer achievement. I like the perfume of these flowers.

And I like her directness, her obvious sincerity, her passion for the truth as Life reveals it to her, and her endeavor to give the reader a swift, vivid picture. She may go very far.

Charles Hanson Towne.

MOODS

MEMORY

Do you know I am living tonight in a cloud of memory? I, who always preach to you of looking forward, am sitting here silently looking backward and tearing the veil from off the dead faces of the past.

Memory is a strange thing, so poignant and alive in its insistence, so dead and lifeless in its reality, so cruel and portentous in its regrets.

It is curious how, merely in the brain, wide vistas of recollection can be opened, and whole pictures of the past stretch before us by simply recalling the touch of a hand, by the stirring of a soft breath of wind, by a sad prolonged street cry, or by the heavy atmospheric pressure of a warm summer's night.

Sometimes it is a strain of music across far waters that brings back long-distant years; again it is the odor of a box suddenly opened, which gives forth the fragrance of violets or rose leaves long since dead and which instantly brings a tug at the heart strings and fills the throat with burning tears.

It seems to me a comparatively easy thing to suppress our memories during the day, when a host of things come clamoring and crowding for us to accomplish.

But the past, with its sad, tragic eyes and fantastic shapes, its shrill, melancholy wails and dear, dead voices, its heavily perfumed flowers, its vibrating, pulsing music, its soft, caressing touches and maddening, heart-rending regrets — these all come filing back one by one and play upon the soul and make the lips turn white. . . .

Sometimes at night!

FAITH

I think it does not matter so much what we believe as what we *want* to believe, — the desire seems to me greater than the accomplishment.

They say "men live by hope," but I feel men must live by faith or else they perish. Or perhaps faith and hope are very closely akin — one being the Touch of God, and the other being the Breath of a Divine Perfume He has tossed out upon the world, so that man might still find a smile where there seemed only to be tears.

Today I do not feel that I am groping my way as I have heretofore done, but a strange exaltation is in me as though a star had caught in my hair, or as if a piece of the moon had come down and brushed against my cheek.

I wonder could you understand if I told you why? If I tell you that for days and nights my soul has been writhing in a cover of darkness, — oppressed by a thousand apprehensions and crushed by the weight of fear? Until today no light has come its way and yet do you know that in that solitude and stillness I have been conscious of a little something stirring in me and trying to make me believe that help *would* come? But the dreariness came again and strange grotesque shapes pressed about me and bade me let go and sink and sink. . . . . . .

Then I lay despairing and could not move or raise my eyes — but suddenly, when my faith had almost ceased to be . . .

God put out His Hand and, stooping down — touched me!

LOVE

It seems absurd I did not recognize it at once, but at first my thoughts were indefinite and I did not know by what name to call it. I had always looked upon it as something so much more personal and individual, and coming this way as it did, it seemed new and strange. It came to me in the subway. I remember it had been raining and as I entered the train I remarked to myself on the hideous smell of damp clothing and dripping umbrellas. At first the crowd was oppressive; I who hate crowds so, shrank a little and tried to gain my balance. It was just then the peculiar thing happened . . .

Suddenly, in spite of the fact that I was pushed and pulled here and there I did not seem to mind. A man rose giving me a seat, and as I sank into it and the crowds thinned out at a station, I looked across the train and saw a woman dozing in the corner. Her face was worn, white and pinched; her clothes dirty and her hat sliding off.

Every time the train swayed her head lurched forward, each second seeming to assume a more uncomfortable position. I looked at her pathetic face and longed with all my heart to put her tired head upon my shoulder, taking my coat and wrapping it around her emaciated form.

Then I looked down the train and saw an old man; he had apparently been to the hospital, because his head was bandaged and his face contracted from time to time in pain. He gazed slyly about, and when he thought no one was looking he spat upon the floor between his legs. Ordinarily I should have wanted to kill him for it, but then, oddly enough, I felt no disgust but only a great pity and sympathy for him.

A small child opposite was screaming shrilly and every few seconds licking the window pane, while his parents fought and argued with each other beside him. I wanted to take their hands and tell them not to quarrel and I longed to take the child on my lap; cuddling it to me and distracting it from the soiled window pane.

Then as I gazed at all the faces along the seats a great understanding and sympathy for them sprang up within me. I wished I could take them by the hand one by one out into the sunlight, giving them what they most desired, and then be able to rejoice at their good fortune in which I would share no part.

I forgot myself completely and a spirit of exaltation came to me such as I had never experienced before. The subway ceased to smell and upon each face and in my heart I seemed to discern a great light. I held my breath while I felt as if I were being carried on by some unknown harmony and rhythm; I was sure that all the eyes in the train had grown kindly and that no one harbored evil in his heart.

Before the feeling faded away — as I knew it would — and left me again my same selfish and miserable self, I longed to ascertain what this sublime mood could be. As I wondered, back from my brain and all the way down to my heart I heard the words beating and hammering my answer —

"This is love!" they cried.

DISGUST

Do you remember the day I left your house so suddenly and rushed out on the street? Or perhaps you do not recall it and did not remark my absence, — you had so many people there, and your house was fragrant with such quantities of flowers, and everyone seemed to pretend at being gay, even if he were not.

And I? I left it all behind me because I heard you boasting in such a light-hearted way of all we had dreamed of and loved so well.

My heart trembled at your careless words and I closed my ears and rushed out before you should have killed my last illusion and made me hate you. Your house, which a few moments before seemed gay and bright, suddenly flung from out its windows the flag of hypocrisy, and became meaningless and empty.

My head ached; and I hurried aimlessly along the street peering into the faces of the passers-by, thinking that in humanity I should find a solace and an answer. . . . But they only pushed and knocked against me and not one spirit spoke to me.

Then I went into the museum and thought that there with art I could find revelation and be comforted. So I walked through the galleries, but I was followed unendingly by the same unsparing mob that jostled me in the streets and suspicious guards glared at me while all around hung low rows of portraits in heterogeneous fashion which, melting into one another, lost their personality and meant nothing to me.

So I dragged myself out again into the spring air and walked wearily toward the park. There, reaching a bench, I sank down and thought at last I could relax undisturbed. But a drunken man came and sat beside me and nudged my elbow, so I rose and moved away and wondered if there were any place in the whole wide world where one could be really alone and unembittered.

Friendship, art and all the things I cherished seemed to have failed me. Suddenly I thought of death!

Then, meditating on the last long sleep, a sense of great peace and the solitude I had longed for came over me . . .

But only for a brief instant, because I remembered with anguish that, even in death, one could not be alone; and the thought of overcrowded and congested cemeteries filled my soul with horror; and I shuddered!

JOY

I looked out of the window at the snow on the ground and something in the sunlight made me throw aside my books and go out.

I do not recall how I reached there, but I found myself in the heart of the park, and maybe because it was so early, or I do not know quite why, — it seemed empty, — I looked across the white stretch of glistening snow and my heart beat with joy at being alone. Suddenly something very odd happened to me:

Everything and everyone in my life seemed to drop away from me; I felt as though my spirit had been freed and as if no harm could ever come to me again.

So I laughed and blew my breath out in the cold air and waved it good-bye, and I shouted aloud and tossed the snow from side to side with my feet. I knew you would be waiting for me and be angry, but that and all things else seemed very remote and far away, so I dismissed it from my mind and did not think of it again.

Then I pretended I was Columbus discovering America and I called out "land ahead." But after, I changed and pretended I was Jeanne d'Arc leading the French army, and all the while sang the Marseillaise because it thrilled me so and I waved my arms and danced.

Then I decided to be the wind, and I ran as fast as I could and fell down in the snow, jumped up again and laughed some more.

I threw kisses and made faces at the sun and I tried to catch the little diamonds that gleamed on the snow, — but each one lured me on to another, until it seemed like an eternal mirage — so I stood still, drew a long breath and thanked God for Life!

Then as I walked on I felt that I possessed everything, because I had youth, health and ambition. And the whole world seemed to be stretching out its alluring hands before me with wonderful rose-tipped fingers!

DESPAIR

One day I said, "There is no such thing as love," and something closed up within me; and although I looked upon people I knew I did not see them. Some horrible apprehension seemed to grip at my heart with ice boned hands. I felt nauseated and sick.

I went home and closed my door and, for the first time in my life, threw my books into a corner and broke my pens and pencils.

After that outburst I sat down and tried to think, but all my thoughts seemed draped in long garbs of black crepe that, stealing in and out through my mind like phantoms on tiptoe, gave me no peace.

I thought what a failure my life had been and I believed every one had deserted me. I longed to die!

I saw your roses, but I threw them on the floor and stepped on them because they seemed fresh and gay; and a thousand sad thoughts rushed through my mind, while I felt as if I were being oppressed by all the nightmares of the world and beating my soul against a closed iron door.

Then I remembered that people said "tears soothe the heart"; so I prayed to be allowed to weep, but instantly cursed myself for praying and cried aloud, "There is no God!"

And all night long I sat in darkness, staring into space with clenched hands, repeating the words over and over again, "No love, no hope" − "No love, no hope" . . .

TENDERNESS

They always said of her that she was selfish and spoiled and that, although she lived in a big house and had everything in the world money could buy, no one really cared about her for herself.

They admitted she had beauty, but they said her face was hard and bitter and that her only power lay in her worldly prosperity, which had a certain empty, insincere following, — but that she had no real influence because she did not have a heart and no one loved her.

I used to hear them talking about her rudeness and her detached indifference, and they seemed to excite themselves greatly about her, and grow angry and shrug their shoulders; then they would always end by thanking God they were not like her.

After these discussions — in which I took no part — I always went home and thought about her. And then one day I went to hear Kreisler play. I think he played more exquisitely than I had ever heard him before; perhaps it was the music of Beethoven that moved me so or, more likely, the mingling of both their spirits that tore so plaintively at my soul.

Whatever the cause, I felt a great spell upon me, and I saw nothing and was not conscious where I was until, suddenly and accidentally, my eyes fell upon her face; I was brought back to my surroundings, — and all the things I had heard about her came to me, and went crowding through my mind.

She was not alone in the box, although she sat apart in a corner, separated from the other people as it seemed to me she always was. She was leaning a bit forward with her hands clasping her knees, her lips a trifle apart and seeming singularly pale; but what I noticed most was the expression in her eyes, which had an entreaty and a pathos in them I had never seen in any face before; — and her mouth was strangely soft with a look of sweetness about its corners.

She was not looking at Kreisler, but gazing out before her as though at something we others could not see, and I was filled with a peculiar sensation that she understood and felt things which were remote from other people.

Then I looked away because somehow I felt as if I were spying at her with her mask off, and looking upon her soul! The violin stopped and, as the last notes vibrated and died away and were swallowed up in the applause, I looked at her again.

Once more the hard look was on her face and the bitter pain in her eyes. I saw the people she was with exchange a casual remark with her, and then draw a little aside and talk among themselves.

All at once a great wave of tenderness came over me, and I longed with sudden eagerness to put my arms about her and draw her to me. I wanted to tell her not to be lonely and sad and bitter, because I knew she was not all they said she was, and all they had made her with their idle talk.

I wanted to hold her hand and tell her I understood and sympathized with her, and that I knew she only seemed all the things they said, simply because no one ever kissed her.

HURT FEELINGS

You remember of course the day I acted so queerly in your studio? How happy we were going up the stairs, and how we laughed and vowed it would be the most wonderful day we had ever spent!

"The day of days," you called it.

And do you remember how I tripped and dropped the tea and sugar packages, and you dropped the cake in an effort to steady me – and how we sat down on the steps and laughed and laughed as though it was the funniest thing in the whole wide world?

And then in the corridor you would not let me open the door until you had kissed my hands.

But as soon as we were in the studio something seemed to snap within me, my mood changed entirely and I ceased to laugh; I put the packages on the table and was very quiet.

Of course you thought I had one of my old-time headaches, and you took out that absurd headache cologne – which never does the slightest bit of good – and insisted upon spraying it over me.

And you tried to make me laugh again and kissed my neck, but in spite of the fact that you looked like an injured little child, I stood looking out of the window and, when you asked me what was the matter, I merely replied "nothing."

Then in the face of all your desperate entreaties I left the studio, and went down the stairs out into the street. . . .

I am sorry now I did it and, although I never meant to tell you the reason — now, because it all seems so trivial, I think I shall:

Do you remember how I stopped laughing the instant you opened the door? That was because I noticed at once the little plant I gave you was placed in a dark corner, withered and dead.

WEARINESS

No, I do not want to dance tonight, nor talk nor play. You think I am foolish because I want to sit here and stare into the night? I wonder! You say I am lazy? I wonder at that too. Well, no matter.

You go and dance and leave me here alone; then when you return you will tell me what you have accomplished by your dancing, and if you feel any the happier for it, — but no, do not bother — I think I shall be too tired even to listen.

It is true you will be exercising your legs, but I shall sit here and travel far and wide among the stars — and exercise my soul.

Do you know my body seems strangely lax tonight? I think I must be quite exhausted; and I am sure that I could sit here for years and years and never move a muscle or enter into life at all again. So tired am I.

Perhaps, if I sit here long enough, all the generations of the future will come and tell me their secrets because they will know I should be far too weary ever to repeat them.

OPPORTUNITY

It is strange how seldom people can judge the psychological moment to reach forth their hands and grasp what they desire. How often does the gardener in the field of life pick the rose before it has really opened or just a little too late, when it has already commenced to fade and drop its petals, — but how divinely fortunate is the one who plucks it just at the right moment and, as a reward, not only has the rose, but very often with it a tiny, glistening, jeweled drop of dew!

We cannot say that this is merely chance, but rather a God-like bit of intuition that is wound about and entwined in some souls.

Too often in our feebleness we say opportunity makes us what we are; and we do not realize our strength or we should say that we will make opportunity for that which *we* wish to be!

I feel that opportunity is something which grows often and plentifully in the lives of some but, like the grass beneath our feet, it is very seldom cultivated and springs up noiselessly and silently so that we do not notice it.

Most of us, when we wish to do something very much or attain a great desire, expect the moment for fulfillment to come heralded with blasts of trumpets — and when it does not come that way, but through an unpretentious medium, we cannot grasp its significance; and so we pass it by . . .

The wise soul is he who expects and seeks opportunity in all places — not graspingly or shrewdly, but silently and with great faith; and who knows and comprehends the law that not always must we go out to seek it, but perhaps, while merely contemplating the stars, will we gain force — and so it will come to us.

Not too obviously, perhaps, but with an interior illumination that will give us the Vision and show us the path onward.

TIME

Time and space mean very little to me today. I am sitting here thinking of ten years ago and marveling because it seems so close and so little forgotten, — infinitely nearer than those moments of even yesterday, which seem already remote and distant.

How strange time is!

Do you know I often fancy that old Father Time holds in his hand some musical instrument? Maybe a harp or a lyre — instead of a scythe as he is always depicted — and he plays and plays and plays . . . mostly very low; and then things that occurred only yesterday seem vague, almost forgotten and far away.

But sometimes he sees our hearts craving to recall vividly some face, to live over again some moment, or to hear once more an almost forgotten echo — and then he takes compassion upon us and he plays madly and loudly, and suddenly, as though in a vision, we witness departed moments; or we see a face or hear a voice close beside us, and so real are they, that we have but to stretch out our hands to touch and caress them, or turn our heads to hear the cadence of a voice rise from out the long-dead past.

Have you noticed how vividly old people recall their childhood?

Ah, that is because Father Time, being so old himself, has a profound attraction for old age, based on reciprocal qualities which he knows them to share in common with him.

So of course he loves them best and, realizing that he has no earthly future to offer them, he draws down his musical instrument and plays louder and louder — and lo! they can sit for hours at a time, slowly rocking backward and forward, and all the while they are living over again some cherished moment and hearing sweet, enchanted music.

And, if you listen closely during the silent intervals between the squeaking and rocking of their chairs, I am sure you will hear them saying softly to themselves as they nod their heads slowly to and fro — "Why, it all seems only yesterday!"

REVELATION

It seems to me that life is absolutely futile and incomplete until we realize that no matter what we are doing, or whither going, it is because of some preconceived reason; and that in the end, when we have reached the last turning of the road and come to lay down our wearying burdens, no matter what our regrets through life may have been — we will know and fully comprehend that the tending of our footsteps this or that way was merely the working out of a great end.

The orientation of our views is so limited and circumscribed that, when something comes to us which we have not desired, we can only feel the bearing down of a cruel fate upon our heads. And too often we toss those same heads back in stubborn despair and grind our teeth in the gale of what must be — thereby losing our balance and sense of what *might* be had we the courage to entwine our strength with that of the Infinite!

Many times the inveiglement of an idea — a set idea which perhaps we have nourished in our hearts for days — will keep us from all realization of the good we might gain by a different shaping of our lives from that which we had dreamed.

To some of us the revelation never comes; and we go on pursuing life with our noses pressed to the ground, without a glimmer of comprehension of the great and superfine machine which marks out and registers our lives.

To others, who are perhaps more worthy, the revelation *does* come, and usually during or after our darkest hours. It is indeed a proof of the Divine that we should receive light after darkness!

To these same it is strange how sometimes it will come slowly like the rising of the moon, and then again quickly as a flood of sunlight after a darkening cloud has passed.

In the sad or desperate moments of our lives when indeed we see nothing to go on for — when we are torn and spent and there seems no end to the coursing of the blood from out our hearts — it is then that the knowledge in a flash comes to us, that there *must* be a reason, and that we could not be made to suffer so without an ultimate beneficial purpose.

And so all striving seems puerile and we cease to beat our wings against the cage, lift our torn hearts instead to the sweet rain of heaven and ask to see the star that may guide us.

And, as small children who, seeing not, obey, so we too, set forth; and, although unconsciously, in our faith become as sages.

FINDING GOD

I have been reading tonight a book on science which, I think, tends to kill all spiritual hope and attributes everything to the material; taking away our dreams of miracles, crushing our hopes in the Beyond and tearing down the belief of a divine intuition within us. It explains all these things as springing entirely from pathological causes and seems to feed the intellect while it starves the Soul. I think so much has been said in this generation about science, so much has been questioned and delved into about it that I cannot help feeling that science will eventually encompass and satiate the world — that is, if we let it engulf us completely and turn our hearts and souls into rocks and machines; and insist in believing that the still silent voice within us, which we once called God, is merely the emotion caused by a craving for food or sleep or air, or some other physical necessity — which will cease when we last close these weary eyes of ours.

It is indeed true to call this the age of science and "The Iron Age," for what could tend to make men's hearts more thoroughly iron than to tell them to stifle and kill all their emotions and that we are, after all, only a part of the scheme of the Whole, and must not look forward because there is no Beyond?

"Where there is no vision the people perish." So in this age when men seek and in answer find only a golden frame − with no color picture inside to brighten the rooms of life − but instead cold dismal facts, perhaps then it is well that thousands of these poor men should be killed off and not taste the bitter poison to the end.

And yet, is it not the irony of fate that science again with its machine guns, its poisoned gas and all other improved and advanced diabolical warfare should be the hand to slay them?

Men's ears that can only listen to the roar of machinery, cannot hear the song of the birds; men's bodies and feet that are so well clothed, cannot feel the clay of the earth nor the poetry of the wind and sun on their bodies; men's eyes that are tired straining in the research room or the laboratory cannot see the stars, and men's hearts that lead themselves into believing that from the decay of these poor bodies there is no future, cannot see God.

And by these words I do not mean to refute the great and everlasting good that science has done for the world, nor do I forget the vast progress for the benefit of humanity in surgery, hygiene and medicine, and the advancement toward comfort, economy of time and manual labor which it has donated to us by the efforts and sacrifices of wonderful and brave men.

To all those who have toiled and still have been able to Believe, I should like to write a eulogy.

But it is to those who, in their search in science, have lost their ideal and come to live so scientifically that their souls, as it were, have dried up and left only the workings of their brains -- it is from these that I would turn my face away. To live *really* it is impossible to live scientifically. We must live by the emotions to survive and find God, because it is only by and through the emotions that we truly palpitate and feel . . . . and reaching out we extend our hands and lean far into the Vast Space of the Infinite!

BRAINSTORM

How absurd people are! As if anyone could ever understand anyone else! I am so tired of people always trying to understand me, when I hold no understanding of myself. Tonight I have no faith and in my brain there are chaos and whirlwinds. I have ceased to believe in God or man.

Do you remember when I used to talk to you of ideals and truth and all such false things? That was when I was quite mad, but tonight I am *sane*; sane and weary of all control and pretenses. I am tired of being polite, of talking low when I wish to shout, of laughing when I want to cry. I am tired of convention and going to dinners and saying "What a charming party this is" when all the while I should like to tear the table-cloth off and smash up the best china.

I am tired of shuffling feet, ever struggling onward and leading nowhere. I am tired of weak vacillating people and those who do not know real love — Love is no love at all where for its sake one is not willing to commit a crime. But I am also tired of loving and of being loved — it seems to be the dark ages since I spoke to you of love — I am tired of lies and truth — more tired of truth since it only raises hopes and in the end fails. How futile all these things are, how misguiding and tragically frail!

If Life only had long hair so that I might run my hand through it and tear it from its roots! If I could only be an earthquake and shake the very civilization of life! Civilization, what a farce! As if there existed any such thing. I wish I could be a hurricane and crush down everything in my way, or a maddening thunderstorm, with its flashes of blood and fire across the sky . . . A thousand dead bodies to-night might lie in my way and I should like to walk over them and, I wish that Life itself were a strip of gauze so that I might tear it asunder and throw it to the winds!

Chaotic wild thoughts are running through my brain, but mostly darkness and a mad desire to end it all. I am so very tired of Life, but most of all I am tired of myself. *Oh, My God*, let me break these chains . . . I am so very tired of myself!

PEACE

It had been such a warm day. Toward sunset do you remember how we stole away to the beach and after driving for some time we finally came to the dunes, got out of the motor and walked the rest of the way?

I can remember now how white the sand was and how our feet sank in it and, when we drew them out again it seemed to cover our tracks leaving hardly any impression behind us. I remember also how the long reeds sprang up and almost hid you from view; then we began to climb the dunes and all out of breath we reached the top, and there below us lay the beach, and the ocean spreading out from it as far as we could see.

I recall catching my breath as I always do when I again perceive the ocean after having been away from it. It always seems to fill me with such inexhaustible wonder and pours into my soul a peculiar strength and power to go on with the dull and terrible things of life . . . forcing me to finish and, at the end, to conquer them. I can see now the blueness of the water and feel again the great stillness that seemed to be about us. Over our left shoulder back of us lay the inlet, with the sun shining on it and causing it to dazzle like a steel needle; and the long thin white beach — like a golden thread — stretching from it and finally seeming to trail off to nothing and burying itself in the foam of the sea.

Do you remember how we lay there forever so long and neither of us said a word? Finally the sun went down and we watched the sand change from gold to red; the sky became violet with little shadings of green and pink and then suddenly — as if by magic — the ocean became quite calm and a fascinating little star appeared reflecting and twinkling on the inlet.

Back on the main land we watched the little lights of the houses come out one by one; in the twilight at first they were very faint and pale, but after as the night stooped down and crept upon us, they grew brighter and stronger.

And then for the first time you broke the silence; turning to me you asked, "What are you feeling?"

I answered "Peace."

TWILIGHT DREAMS

As I open the long windows and step out upon the terrace, the presence of the mysterious hour is upon me . . . A strange undefined blue mist rises from the earth and gently, like a magical veil, winds itself around the trees and slowly rising, presses its face against the sky as though to peer into the eyes, and read the heart of the stars.

Fantastic trees dimly outlined, bend together and whisper softly; suddenly I feel as though the air were charged with all the wishes of the world. Great and small, joyous and sad wishes, all thrown out from the struggling desirous heart of Life and, at twilight hour stealing silently — some a little ashamed, some a little proud — to nestle under the white moon — flowers in hopes that some soul of the dead — which steal about at twilight hour too — may be their friend and help them to come true.

Timidly, and trembling a little from the embraces of the mist, a tiny star shines out, while slowly and reverently the darkness kneels down and kisses the face of the earth. A vast and deep silence has come over everything; and I, with all else, find myself holding my breath as I steal back into the room and sink into a chair. Leaning back languidly I half close my eyes, while far off I smell the salt and sadness of the sea . . . Weirdly and ghostlike you creep in and, in my twilight dreams, you come to me!

SACRED FIRE:
A MINOR POET'S LEGACY

Like a starry-eyed lover tangled in a secret affair, Mercedes de Acosta wrote *Moods* furtively and passionately. Of her young self, she later said: "I was really only interested in writing, which I did at night – often starting at midnight and ending in the early hours of the morning." Her mother, an intensely Catholic heiress who was by that time a widow, did not approve.[1]

Mercedes filled her daytime hours in 1910s New York with working openly and fiercely for women's suffrage, as well as taking a nurse's aide course – which she hated – and otherwise navigating as best she could the expectations of a wealthy socialite. In the early 1920s, she published three volumes of poetry in three years – and then no more.

As poet Sharon Olds said, "anyone who blooms at all, ever, is very lucky."[2] Instead of a late bloomer like Olds, an aster or an autumn rose, Mercedes as a poet was a spring ephemeral – a wine-red trillium hidden in the woods but boldly radiating a distinctive scent – or a bright red tulip, striking in color and mesmerizing even as she turned herself inside out.

In many ways, Mercedes both lived and wrote unconventionally, like the bright red tulip at the moment when its petals open so much that they contradict themselves, morphing from a cup shape into a star.

*

Some facts about her fascinating life.

Mercedes de Acosta was born in New York City in 1892 or 1893,[3] the youngest of eight children. Her mother came from "ancient and noble Castilian families,"[4] and her father was a Cuban businessman who had narrowly escaped execution by firing squad for organizing a revolt. Mercedes grew up on the West Side of Manhattan at a time when horse-drawn coaches traveled the avenues, with a future U.S. president, an ambassador and a financier among her neighbors.

She was sensitive, thoughtful, ardent and often lonely. In her memoir, *Here Lies the Heart*, she describes her beginnings as a writer:

> As soon as I could read and write I read every book I could possibly lay my hands on

no matter how much over my head the contents seemed to be. It would be more truthful to say I devoured them, so ferocious was my longing for knowledge. Wallowing in the poets, I too began to write poetry.[5]

From a young age, Mercedes was acquainted with creative people and influential culture makers. Her strikingly gorgeous and extravagant sister, Rita de Acosta Lydig, took her to visit "many great artists in Paris." As she recalled:

> [Rita] treated me like a grownup and used to introduce me then as her "canary" . . . I met Rodin . . . Edith Wharton . . . Sarah Bernhardt . . . and many others — some with less celebrated names but burning, nevertheless, the *feu sacré* within their hearts as brightly as the more famous ones who had, in the worldly sense, succeeded.[6]

Mercedes also had formative experiences of love — the main subject of her poetry — outside the mainstream. While briefly attending a Catholic school, she carried love letters between two nuns and then witnessed their heartbreaking, forced separation. This led her to "weeping hysterically . . . sobbing wildly . . . and beating [her] head against the wall."[7]

On a happier note, she was befriended in childhood by the owner of a Broadway theater. For a time, she spent Sunday afternoons with him and his mistress, an actress. Those visits came to an end when Mercedes's mother accidentally tipped off the man's neglected wife, but she was still allowed to "go with him backstage to matinées," where she "learned to know and love the people of the theater and to feel at home with them."[8]

Mercedes knew and loved *people of the theater* as a whole and in the abstract, as well as individually and intimately in the flesh. Before, during, and after her fifteen-year marriage to painter and Army captain Abram Poole, she was romantically involved with many beautiful actresses and dancers including Alla Nazimova, Isadora Duncan, Eva Le Gallienne, Marlene Dietrich, and Greta Garbo.[9] She adamantly refused to take her husband's name as her own, and she wore – and encouraged her lovers to wear – pants at times instead of skirts.

In addition to her poetry collections and two published novels, Mercedes wrote numerous plays and screenplays; writing for stage and screen was her focus for several decades. But while four of her plays were produced and well-received, others were never staged, and her screenplays similarly went unproduced.[10] According to biographer Robert A. Schanke, "with the exception of her 1960 autobiography, her last forty years were devoid of any literary accomplishment. The early promise she had shown . . . never truly materialized."[11]

This was not a mystery or accident. Mercedes's tastes were unbridled and edgy; both she and her writing made people uncomfortable. Perhaps emboldened by the class privilege and financial security she enjoyed for most of her life, she chose the path of less recognition but more truth.

Schanke describes her "cloying emotionalism . . . and fanaticism . . . clouding her vision, taste and artistic decisions," saying she "was blinded by sexual passion."[12] But I prefer scholar Bridget Marie Sundin's assertion that "there is something powerful to be gained in reframing Mercedes's 'failure' to become a successful writer as more accurately being a sapphic woman's successful act of resistance against sexist, homophobic and heteronormative societal standards."[13]

As she neared the end of her career, Mercedes wrote in – and of – her memoir, "How am I to convey to the reader the diverse people I feel within me?"[14] It's a question she pursued for many years, beginning with the internal contradictions and wild vacillations of *Moods*.

*

Here is Mercedes's recollection of publishing *Moods*, describing it about forty years later:[15]

> The winter of 1918–19 was a memorable one for me. Howard Cook, the young, progressive and enthusiastic editor of a small publishing house . . . was well regarded in the literary world . . . So I gathered up my courage one day and, with two manuscripts under my arm . . . went down to call on him. I consulted no one. In fact, no one knew I had written them.
>
> . . . He gave me a slender volume of Sara Teasdale's poems . . . remarking as he did so that he considered her, Edna St. Vincent Millay and Elinor Wylie the three best modern American poets . . . Then he charmingly added, "Perhaps after I read your poems, they will be included in my choice."
>
> "Oh, I will never be anything but a minor poet," said I.

"Great poets are the rarest thing in the world. Minor poets can, nevertheless, give much in their own way. Go on working, regardless of what you think of your work. Don't worry about your poetic rank – great, minor or zero. Just let your verses flow without feeling self-conscious about them."

With this good advice, I left his office.

*

Reading *Moods*, I am warmly drawn in by the unabashed sincerity of the speaker's voice, especially when Mercedes uses direct address. Beginning with the question "Do you know I am living tonight in a cloud of memory?" is so intimate – especially since this is not a rhetorical question but is immediately followed by "I, who always preach to you . . .", which indicates a specific, imagined listener.

I love that she perceived such depth of meaning in details like a withered potted plant, and inferred from an unguarded face taking in a concert that the listener suffered "simply because no one ever kissed her." Instead of objectively describing an interaction or creating a scene that would play out as on a stage, Mercedes's speaker invites readers to step into the role of her friend, her confidant, her beloved.

Harriet Monroe, founder of the journal *Poetry*, wrote of *Moods*: "There is genuine feeling in these little human vignettes, a situation is often vividly and picturesquely presented."[16] She published seven other poems by Mercedes, and the two corresponded regarding edits. Monroe's letters to Mercedes have not survived, but what she received from the young poet shows that Mercedes sent her poetry books, novels and new poem submissions for about ten years. In one letter Mercedes said, "I have been trying to write with more care and remember your advice."[17] And later, "Your opinion is very stimulating to me."[18]

Clearly, Mercedes valued poetry – both reading and writing it. She had a strong beginning as a published poet, following *Moods* with *Archways of Life* (1921) and *Streets and Shadows* (1922). So why did she stop?

In her memoir, abruptly inserted between descriptions of Rita's beau and their mother's death, is a passage that describes the end of Mercedes' poetry career but does not elaborate on her decision:

Until 1931 poems of mine were published in *Poetry* magazine and several of them were read over the radio, but after these I never submitted another. I felt that there were already enough minor poets in the world. After that I decided to write poems for myself but never again for publication.[19]

In 1928, she wrote to Monroe that the publisher of her second novel, *Until the Day Break*, had "promised to bring out a new book of verse of mine,"[20] but evidently that did not happen. I can imagine she experienced negative reactions to her poems that made her turn toward stage writing instead. Poetry, as Tracy K. Smith has said, is soul language.[21] Given the frankness and candor of Mercedes's writing, it seems likely she tired of — or may have feared — baring her soul in public. In playwriting, her same-sex love and gender nonconformity could be presented in coded ways or given plausible deniability within stories of historical figures such as Joan of Arc.

Schanke points out that *Until the Day Break* came out the same year as Radclyffe Hall's *The Well of Loneliness*. He posits that "the public outrage against lesbian themes convinced Mercedes that she could never again write as openly as she had been accustomed."[22] Although she stopped *publishing*, she continued *writing* poems, such as a privately printed collection dedicated to set designer Gladys Calthrop.[23]

In a way, despite their different personalities, Mercedes may have felt similar to her predecessor Emily Dickinson, who *published* few poems but *wrote* for many decades within and for an intimate social world that was more understanding, more to her liking, safer.

*

What is Mercedes's legacy?

She wrote bravely of matters of the heart at a time when it was unsafe for her to do so. And she adopted an earnest style that contrasts potently with many – often male – writers' abhorrence of sentimentality. Her prose poems realize Charles Baudelaire's ambition to create "poetic prose . . . supple enough and rugged enough to adapt itself to the lyrical impulses of the soul, the undulations of reverie, the jibes of conscience."[24]

I agree with Charles Hanson Towne that these "fragments . . . stand out in one's reading in refreshing contrast to many opaque books of verse." And I love knowing that over a hundred years ago, a young queer Latina wrote them furtively but with a commitment and sincerity that still shines out of these little rectangles.

Minor poet or otherwise, Acosta certainly burned with the sacred fire she recognized in others. Introducing her, Towne wrote: "She may go very far." Perhaps in a parallel universe she did.

Or perhaps she will.

KATHRYN GOOD-SCHIFF.

ENDNOTES

1. Acosta, Mercedes de. *Here Lies the Heart*. 1960. Reprint, Mansfield Centre, CT: Martino Publishing, 2016, 76.

2. *The Writer's Almanac With Garrison Kiellor*. "Words From the Front by Ron Padgett." Minnesota Public Radio, November 19, 2007. https://writersalmanac.publicradio.org/index.php%3Fdate=2007%252F11%252F19.html.

3. Schanke, Robert A. *That Furious Lesbian: The Story of Mercedes de Acosta*. Uncorrected proof. Southern Illinois University Press, 2003, 181.

4. Acosta. *Here Lies the Heart*, 7.

5. Acosta. *Here Lies the Heart*, 34.

6. Acosta. *Here Lies the Heart*, 47.

7. Acosta. *Here Lies the Heart*, 36.

8. Acosta. *Here Lies the Heart*, 5.

9. Cohen, Lisa. "Fame Fatale." *Out*, October 1999.

10. Hunt, Kristin. "Story of a Pioneering Queer Writer's Audacious Love Life Is Preserved in the Rosenbach Collection." *PhillyVoice*, October 5, 2023. https://www.phillyvoice.com/rosenbach-museum-mercedes-de-acosta-lgbtq-writer-inside-the-archives/.

11. Schanke. *That Furious Lesbian*, 173.

12. Schanke, Robert A. "Say What You Will About Mercedes de Acosta." In *Staging Desire: Queer Readings of American Theater History*, edited by Kim Marra and Robert A. Schanke, 81–104. University of Michigan Press, 2002.

13. Sundin, Bridget Marie. "'I Adore You Forever': The Performative Past of Mercedes de Acosta and Marlene Dietrich." Abstract. 2023. https://iucat.iu.edu/catalog/21092358.

14. Acosta. *Here Lies the Heart*, 210.

15. Acosta. *Here Lies the Heart*, 101–102.

16. Monroe, Harriet. "Review: A Score of First Books." *Poetry* 17, No. 5 (February 1921), 276–87.

17. Acosta, Mercedes de. Letter to Harriet Monroe, July 1920. From *Poetry: A Magazine of Verse*. Records, [Box 6, Folder 14], Hanna Holborn Gray Special Collections Research Center, University of Chicago Library.

18. Acosta, Mercedes de. Letter to Harriet Monroe, December 9, 1920. From *Poetry: A Magazine of Verse*. Records, [Box 6, Folder 14].

19. Acosta. *Here Lies the Heart*, 135.

20. Acosta, Mercedes de. Letter to Harriet Monroe, May 7, 1928. From *Poetry: A Magazine of Verse*. Records, [Box 6, Folder 14].

21. Smith, Tracy K. *Ordinary Light: A Memoir*. New York: Alfred A. Knopf, 2015.

22. Schanke. "Say What You Will About Mercedes de Acosta."

23. Barnett, David. "Mercedes de Acosta: The Poet Who Had Affairs With the 20th Century's Most Famous Women." *The Guardian*, March 2, 2024. https://www.theguardian.com/books/2024/mar/02/mercedes-de-acosta-the-poet-who-had-affairs-with-the-20th-centurys-most-famous-women.

24. Baudelaire, Charles. *Paris Spleen*. Translated by Louise Varèse. New Directions, 1970, ix–x.

Mercedes de Acosta

COLOPHON

The typography and layout of the original edition by Moffat, Yard and Co. is problematic. It appears that the compositor worked from Mercedes's typescript and set the manuscript as verse and not as prose. While the typescript of the manuscript does not exist anymore, it appears as if the compositor was attempting to match each line of typescript prose as the equivalent of a typeset line of verse. The run-on of some long typescript lines once set as type would be brought down to the next line and indented (but not always). Following lines would be typeset flush left. The end result was a visual mess that does not quite meet the standards of prose layout nor does it meet the standards of verse layout. Extant mentions by the author and others convey the sense that *Moods* was intended to be a book of prose vignettes. The publication of "Opportunity" in a mention of the book in a publication contemporaneous with the book's publication reveals that the vignette was typeset as prose with normal paragraph indents and extra space between paragraphs. That more customary layout of prose is used herein. (Ironically, the appearance of "Opportunity" in that publication ran under the headline "New York Society Woman Writes Free Verse.") Such manglings of prose poetry by well-meaning compositors, and publishers, are unfortunately common enough through the history and development of the prose poem.

quale [kwa-lay]:   *Eng.* n.
1. A property (such as hard-
ness) considered apart from
things that have that prop-
erty. 2. A property that is
experienced as distinct from
any source it may have in a
physical object. *Ital.* pron.a.
1. Which, what. 2. Who. 3.
Some. 4. As, just as.